Practical Guide to the Operational Use of the PPS-43 Submachine Gun

By Erik Lawrence

Copyright ©2014 Erik Lawrence

I0160083

Printed and bound in the United States of America

First printing 2012
Second Printing 2014

ISBN 10: 1-941998-06-2
ISBN 13: 978-1-941998-06-9
EBOOK-ISBN 13: 978-1-941998-25-0
LCCN: Not Yet Assigned

ATTENTION US MILITARY UNITS, US GOVERNMENT AGENCIES, AND PROFESSIONAL ORGANIZATIONS: Quantity discounts are available on bulk purchases of this book. Special books or book excerpts can also be created to fit specific needs. For information, please contact:

Erik Lawrence
www.vig-sec.com   erik@vig-sec.com

Firearms are potentially dangerous and must be handled responsibly by individuals. The technical information presented in this manual on the use of the PPS-43 Submachine Gun reflects the author's research, beliefs, and experiences. The information in this book is presented for academic study only. Neither the author nor the publisher assumes any responsibility for the use or misuse of information contained in this book.

SAFETY NOTICE
Before starting an inspection, ensure the weapon is cleared. Do not manipulate the trigger until the weapon has been cleared of all ammunition. Inspect the chamber to ensure that it is empty and no ammunition is present. Keep the weapon oriented in a safe direction when loading and handling.

AMMUNITION NOTICE- This weapon fires the 7.62x25mm (Tokarev), not the 9x19mm NATO (9mm Luger) or 9x18mm (Makarov). Firing the incorrect ammunition will damage the weapon and possibly injure the operator.

Training should be received from knowledgeable and experienced operators on this particular weapons system. Vigilant Security Services, LLC provides this training and continually perfects its instruction with up-to-date information from actual use.

www.vig-sec.com

PREFACE

This manual is intended to be a reference for those involved in the use, maintenance and instruction of the featured firearm. My aim in writing these manuals is to set the record straight and dispel many of the false assumptions related to the different firearms. The early sections of the manual contain background material on the featured firearm which allows the user to gain the basic building blocks for further education. The firearms featured in these manuals have been used for decades by our allies and enemies, and will be for the foreseeable future, so why are we not experts with them? If I am fighting with the firearm or providing instruction on a firearm, I want to use and know their system better than they do.

The rationale for writing these manuals comes from the fact that there are not libraries of easily accessible references to use in developing your own training system for these firearms. Many of the old military field manuals are decades old and were incorrectly translated by someone who had no idea what the firearm could do, let alone basic firearm knowledge. We started from the ground up and developed the manuals to provide instruction in progressive steps that could be easily grasped and continually referred back to. A good grounding in the basics of firearms, safety, and instruction allows the user to use these manuals to their maximum value. A competent user will find little difficulty in interpreting and applying the information in the manual to their own training program.

The guide goes through the most fundamental parts of the firearm in detail and more advanced techniques are not covered as extensively. With this in mind the user can use these principles and adapt it as needed to their required level of instruction. The emphasis of this guide is in acquiring familiarity with the fundamentals of all firearms and learned competence rather than becoming a firearms guru.

Many of the points in these guides were developed from scratch in theatres of conflict and are continually improved and updated for each edition. I have continually used vetted points from users and professionals in the guides to continually update them to the best known practices for each particular firearm. If it is valid and relevant we will include it in the next edition.

Please note that this guide assumes some familiarity with the basic concepts in firearm safety, gun handling skills, common sense and an ability to process new information. Readers should have knowledge of the difference in calibers, countries of origin, and the knowledge of the priority of the skills needed for development.

I hope you find this work useful and remember that a manual does not replace proper training and hands on experience. Please email comments to erik@vig-sec.com, particularly if you find any errors or glaring omissions.

Erik Lawrence

Table of Contents

Section 1..1

  Introduction 1

    Background...1

    Nomenclature 5

    Operation...6

Section 2..8

  Maintenance 8

  Clearing the PPS-43 SMG...9

  Disassembling the PPS-43 SMG..12

  Cleaning the PPS-43 14

  Reassembling the PPS-43 SMG...17

  Performing a Function Check on the PPS-43 SMG 19

Section 3..20

  Operation and Function...20

    Loading the PPS-43 Stick Magazine 20

    Loading the Stick Magazine in a PPS-43 SMG......................................20

    Firing the PPS-43 SMG 22

    Zeroing the PPS-43 SMG 25

Section 4..27

  Performance Problems...27

    Malfunction Procedures 27

Appendix A – Ammunition Specifics...29

Appendix B – Ammunition Comparison..36

Appendix C - Munitions Packaging Markings 37

Appendix D – Manufacturer ID Markings 40

Appendix E – Non-Standard Weapons Theory..42

PPS-43

SUBMACHINE
GUN

Section 1

Introduction

The objective of this manual is to allow the reader to be able to use the Sudayev-designed PPS-43 submachine gun (SMG) competently. The manual will give the reader background/specifications of the weapon; instructions on its operation, disassembly, and assembly; proper firing procedure; and malfunction/misfire procedures. Operator-level maintenance will also be detailed to allow the reader to understand and become competent in the use and maintenance of the PPS-43 SMG.

Figure 1-1 PPS-43 SMG with stock folded

Background

The **PPS** (Russian: *ППС - Пистолет-пулемёт Судаева* or *Pistolet-pulemjot Sudaeva*, in English: "Sudayev's submachine-gun") was a series of Soviet submachine guns in the 7.62x25mm Tokarev caliber developed by Alexei Sudayev as a low-cost personal defense weapon for reconnaissance units, vehicle crews, and support-service personnel.

The PPS and its variants were used extensively by the Soviet Red Army during World War II and were later adopted by the armed forces of several countries of the former Warsaw Pact as well as its many proxy forces.

The PPS was created in response to a Red Army requirement for a compact and lightweight weapon that would provide similar accuracy and firepower (with a reduced rate of fire) while utilizing a more cost-effective means of production than the Soviet PPSh-41 submachine gun being widely deployed at the time. During the design phase, emphasis was placed on simplifying the production process and eliminating most machining operations; sheet-steel stamping was selected to make most of the weapon's parts. These cost-saving measures reduced the amount of machined components to a bare minimum, cutting down machining time by more than half (2.7 hours of machining required to complete a PPS as opposed to 7.3 hours for the PPSh-41). Savings of over 50% were also noted in terms of raw steel usage (13.7 lb/6.2 kg instead of 30 lb/13.9 kg) and the number of workers, required to fabricate the individual components and conduct final assembly of the weapon.

Prototypes were evaluated successfully during the spring of 1942, after which the firearm was accepted into service later that year as the PPS-42. The weapon was put into small-scale production during the Siege of Leningrad; mass production did not commence until early 1943 at the Sestroryetsk Arsenal (over 45,000 weapons were produced before being replaced by the improved PPS-43). The improvements to production efficiency allowed the Soviets to increase monthly submachine gun output from 135,000 units to 350,000 weapons.

Captured PPS-43s were used by the Germans as the MP719(r). Unlike with PPSh-41, captured examples were not converted to fire 9mm Parabellum rounds. However, a slightly modified copy of PPS-43 was produced in Finland under designation m44, and it used a 9mm cartridge; 10,000 examples were produced. After the war, it was license-produced in small numbers in West Germany and Spain. It was also given to and copied by several Soviet client states.

The characteristics of the Soviet PPS-43 SMG

Figure 1-2 PPS-43

A. Country of Origin: USSR/Russia

B. Military Designation: *Pistolet Pulemyot Sudayeva* obr 1943G (PPS-43)

C. Operation: Full-automatic fire

D. Cartridge: 7.62x25mm Soviet Tokarev

E. Ammunition:

    a. Type P1; 86-grain bullet, 8-gram charge

    Muzzle Velocity: 1500 fps

    b. Type P-41; 74-grain bullet, 8-gram charge, AP/Incendiary

    Muzzle Velocity: 1600 fps

F. Length:

    a. Stock Folded: 24.2 in (615mm)

    b. Stock Extended: 32.3 in (820mm)

G. Barrel: 9.6 in (243mm), 4-groove, right-hand twist

H. Weight

    a. SMG: 6.7 lbs. (3kg) Unloaded

    b. Stick magazine – 35 rounds:

        i. Loaded- 1.5 lbs. (.7 kg)

        ii. Unloaded- .7 lbs (.3 kg)

I. Type of Feed: 35-round detachable box

J. Operating System: Blowback, open bolt

K. Rate of Fire: 600 to 800 rpm

L. Maximum Effective Range: 200 meters

The PPS-43 is a full-automatic-only weapon based on simple blowback principle and is fired from the open bolt. The safety is located at the front of the triggerguard. The receiver and barrel shroud are made from stamped steel. Rear sight is an L-shaped flip type and is marked for 100 and 200 meters distance; the front sight is a fixed-blade type. The barrel is equipped with a simple muzzle brake/compensator to manage muzzle rise. The folding stock is made from steel and folds up and over the top of the receiver. Barrel was chrome-lined and thus very durable -- average barrel life was 20,000 rounds.

NOTE -- PPS-43 used only one type of magazine – a curved box magazine, which held 35 rounds. These magazines were externally similar to, but NOT compatible with a box magazines of PPSh-41.

Nomenclature

Figure 1-3 Photo of the overall PPS-43 SMG

1- Buttstock
2- Firing Grip
3- Stock Release Button
4- Operating Handle
5- Rear Sight

6- Ejection Port
7- Barrel Heat Shield
8- Protected Front Sight
9- Muzzle/Compensator
10- Magazine in well

11- Magazine Release Lever
12- Safety
13- Trigger

Stick Magazine Nomenclature

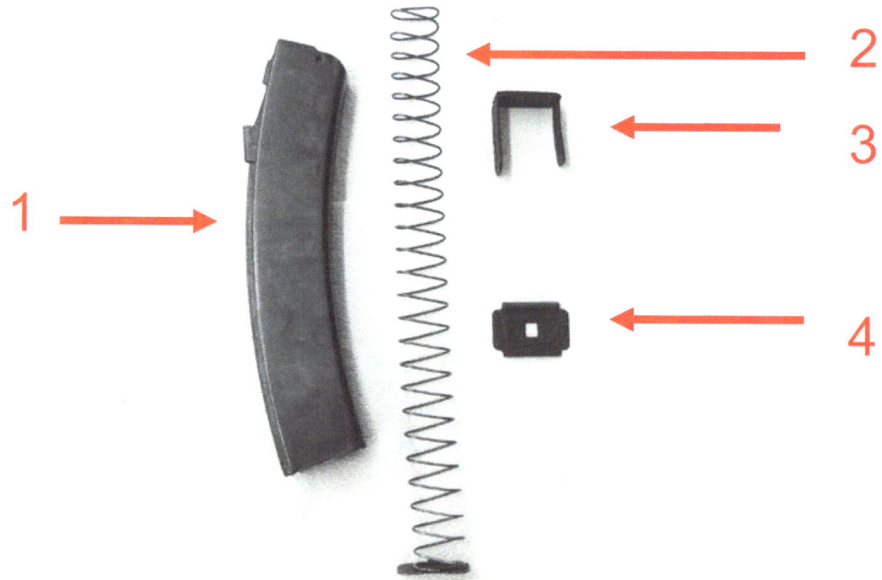

Figure1-4 Stick magazine nomenclature

1- Body   2- Spring   3- Follower   4- Floorplate

Operation

The safety is on the right side of the forward part of the trigger guard; forward is "FIRE" and to the rear is "SAFE" (Figures 1-5 and 1-6).

Safety and Bolt Positions

NOTE- Remember that the PPS-43 is a fixed-firing pin open-bolt firing weapon. You must remove the source of ammunition (magazines) to clear the weapon safely. Riding the bolt forward to close the bolt on a weapon with a loaded magazine will cause the weapon to fire!

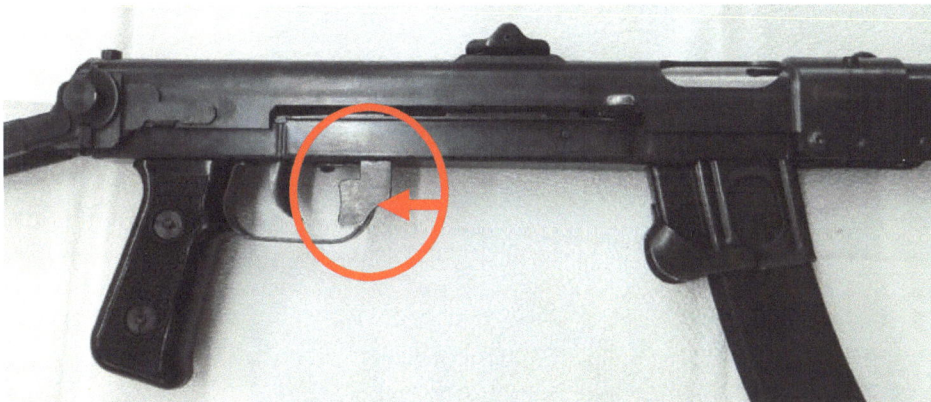

Figure 1-5 Safety engaged and the bolt is forward on an empty chamber.

1. Empty chamber or dud round in chamber- Safety position is engaged, and the bolt is fully forward on an empty chamber or dud round (Figure 1-5).

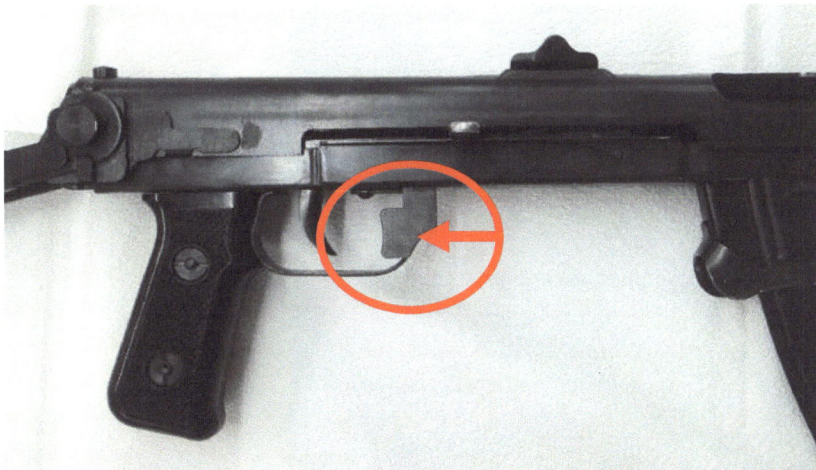

Figure 1-6 Safety is engaged to the rear, and bolt is retracted fully to the rear.

2. Safety position is engaged, and the bolt is retracted fully to the rear (Figure 1-6). This is a safety/bolt position for the weapon when preparing to fire or contact is imminent. Care must be taken when carrying the PPS-43 in this configuration

as there is a danger of accidental firing as a result of dropping or jarring the weapon enough to disengage the safety catch; the bolt could be spring driven forward to fire. To remove the weapon from this configuration without firing the weapon, remove the magazine and properly clear the weapon and return the safety/bolt to the safe storage condition, bolt forward on an empty chamber and on "SAFE".

Figure 1-7 Safety is not engaged, and the bolt is retracted fully to the rear ready to fire.

3. Safety position is not engaged, and the bolt is retracted fully to the rear ready to fire (Figure 1-7). This is a safety/bolt position for the weapon when actually firing. Care must be taken when carrying the PPS-43 in this configuration as there is a danger of accidental firing as a result of dropping or jarring the weapon enough to disengage the trigger bar; and the bolt could be spring driven forward to fire. To remove the weapon from this configuration after firing, you must properly clear the weapon and return the safety/bolt to the safe storage configuration as noted in paragraph #1 of this section.

Section 2

Maintenance

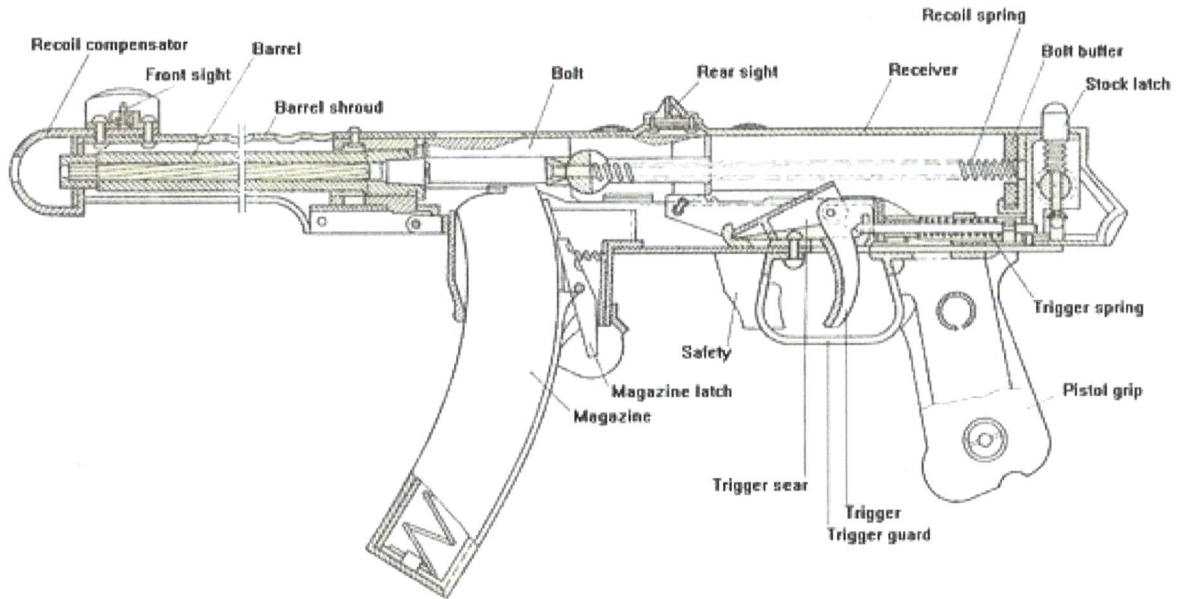

Figure 2-1 Cutaway sketch of PPS-43 internal mechanisms

Clearing the PPS-43 SMG

Figure 2-2a Bolt to the rear   **Figure 2-2b Bolt forward**
PPS-43 SMG safety catch position SAFE

A. Ensure the SMG is on "SAFE," the safety is to the rear in the triggerguard, and the SMG is pointed in a safe direction (Figures 2-2a and 2-2b).

Figure 2-3a Releasing the magazine

Figure 2-3b Removing the magazine

B. Remove the magazine by pressing the magazine release lever towards the magazine (forward) (Figure 2-3a) and pull the magazine from the magazine well (Figure 2-3b). Place the magazine in a magazine pouch or set it down.

Figure 2-4 Ready to fire

C. Place the SMG on 'FIRE' and pull the bolt to the rear if not already retracted (Figure 2-4).

Figure 2-5 Empty chamber

D. Look in the ejection port to inspect the chamber visually to ensure there is no round in the chamber that failed to be extracted and ejected (Figure 2-5).

Figure 2-6 Lowering the bolt onto an empty chamber

E. If you have ensured the magazine is removed and the chamber is clear, while holding rearward pressure on the operating handle, press the trigger and allow the bolt to move slightly forward. Once the bolt has moved forward 1/4", let go of the trigger and continue to allow the bolt to move forward under your control (Figure 2-6).

Disassembling the PPS-43 SMG

NOTE- Place the SMG's parts on a flat, clean surface with the muzzle oriented in a safe direction.

When the operator begins to disassemble the SMG, it should be done in the following order:

Figure 2-7a Press receiver release   **2-7b pivot the upper portion**

1. Press in on the spring-loaded receiver release and swing the upper receiver down by pressing down on the forward heatshield (Figures 2-7a & 2-7b).

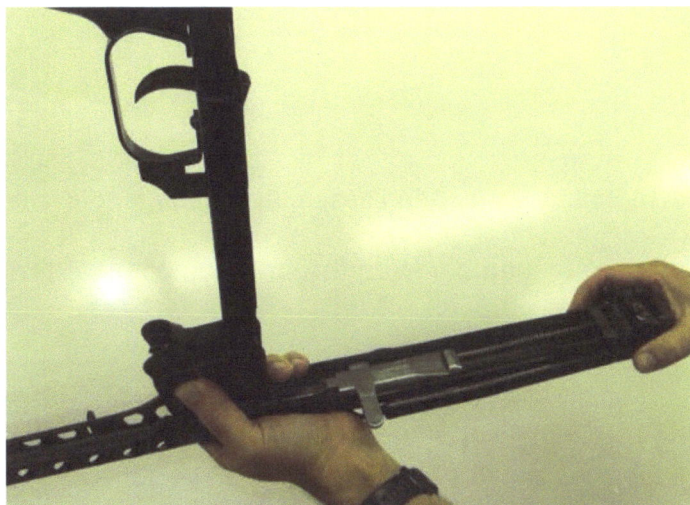

Figure 2-8 removing the bolt assembly

2. Turn the SMG upside down to pull the operating handle rearward and raise it up on the front of the bolt (Figure 2-8).

Figure 2-9

3. Press the bolt, driving spring assembly, and buffer rearward, then up and out of the receiver by lifting up on the front of the bolt or charging handle (Figure 2-9).

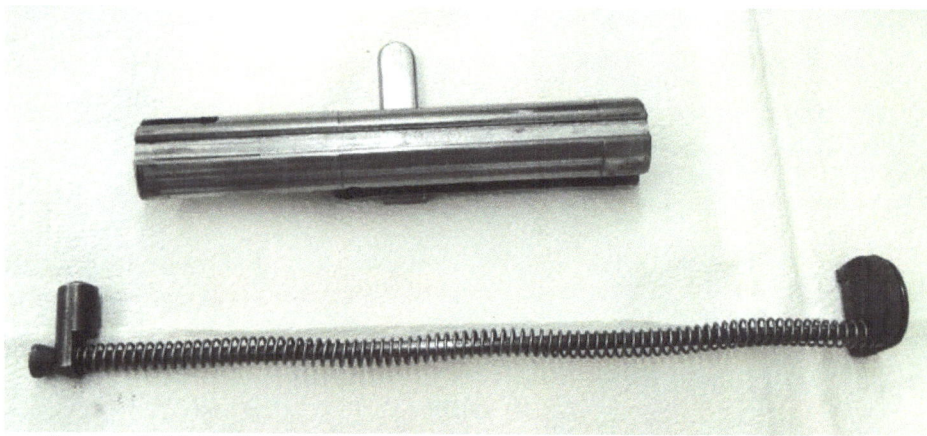

Figure 2-10 Bolt, driving spring assembly and buffer disassembled

4. Pull the driving spring assembly from the bolt and remove the buffer (Figure 2-10).

Cleaning the PPS-43

Figure 2-11 Photo of the weapon parts

1. Once fully dissembled into the major groups (stock and receiver, bolt, driving spring assembly, and buffer), clean each individual part with a powder solvent (Figure 2-11).

2. Clean the bolt, driving spring assembly, and buffer with a powder solvent and dry when completed.

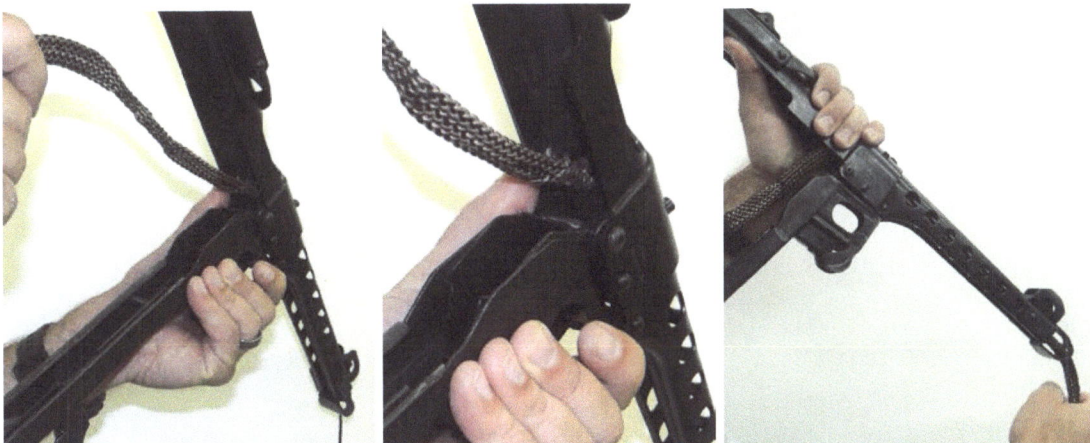

Figure 2-12a-c Photos of the Boresnake pulled through bore

3. Clean the barrel with the cleaning rods that are stored in the hollow section of the buttstock(Figure 2-12a-c). Use solvent-lubricated brass brushes to break up carbon in the bore, and then use a solvent-covered patch to push the carbon out and then a dry patch until clean. The bores are chrome lined, so they clean up easily. A bore snake is a great bore-cleaning product to do this as the barrel is clean with one pass of the bore snake. Bore snake for the 7.62 caliber is item number VSS-240115.

Figure 2-13
Photo of the muzzle and compensator

4. Cleaning of the exterior of the muzzle and compensator is required as corrosive ammo can greatly affect it because it is not chromed. Copious amounts of powder solvent and time to allow it to break down the carbon are suggested. Once it is broken down, wipe until clean (Figure 2-13).

5. Once all parts are cleaned, they should be inspected for damage. Points to inspect are the condition of the front and rear sights, fixed firing pin, driving spring assembly, buffer, and overall condition of all internal parts.

6. Prior to reassembling of the SMG, a light coat of protective oil should be applied to all metal surfaces. Grease should be lightly applied to all the metal surfaces that make contact in the operation of the weapon.

Disassembling the Stick Magazine

Figure 2-14a Depress floorplate lock

Figure 2-14b Remove floorplate

1. Use a pointed object to depress the retaining plate through the floor plate and start to slide the floor plate to the rear. The older, dirtier, and/or rusty the magazine is, the harder this step will be to do. Be careful not to slide the floor plate fully off until you are ready to apply pressure to the retainer plate, as it is under spring tension (Figures 2-14a and 2-14b).

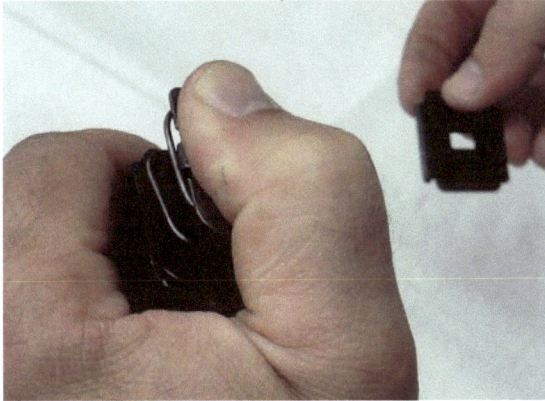

Figure 2-15a Capture spring tension

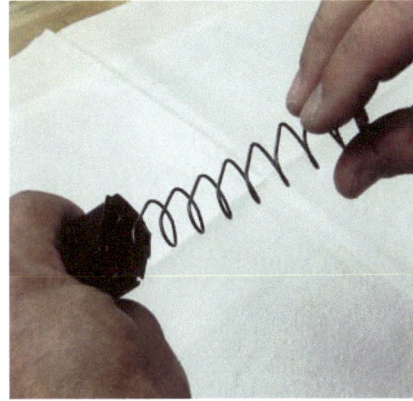

Figure 2-15b Release tension and remove spring and follower

2. Once you have the floor plate started, use your thumb to hold the retainer plate and remove the floor plate fully. Now you can release the spring tension in a controlled manner and remove the spring and follower from the magazine body. The follower and retaining plate can be removed from the spring if needed for thorough cleaning (Figures 2-15a and 2-15b).

NOTE- It is very important to clean the inside of the magazine body and the outside of the follower. Keep the magazine as dry as possible but lightly coated with a protectant to prevent rusting.

3. To reassemble, just reverse the process.

Reassembling the PPS-43 SMG

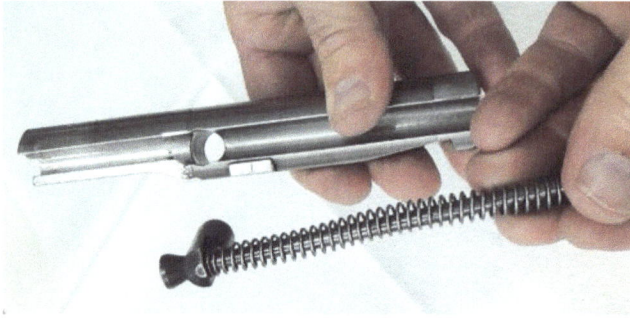

Figure 2-16a

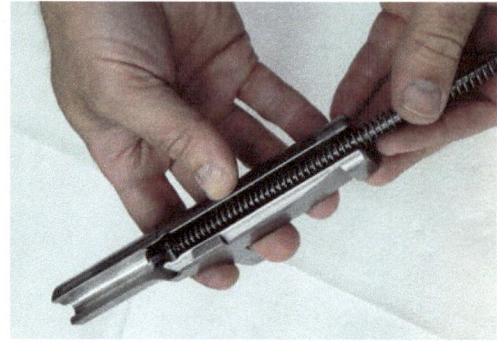

Figure 2-16b

1. Insert the driving spring assembly into the bolt and rotate the buffer so the flat side is up (Figures 2-16a and 2-16b).

Figure 2-17a

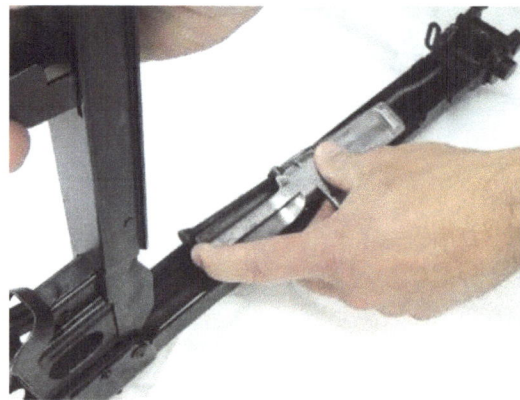

Figure 2-17b

2. Place the rounded side of the buffer and spring assembly into the rear of the upper receiver (Figure 2-17a). Pull the bolt back to swing it down into position in the receiver (Figure 2-17b).

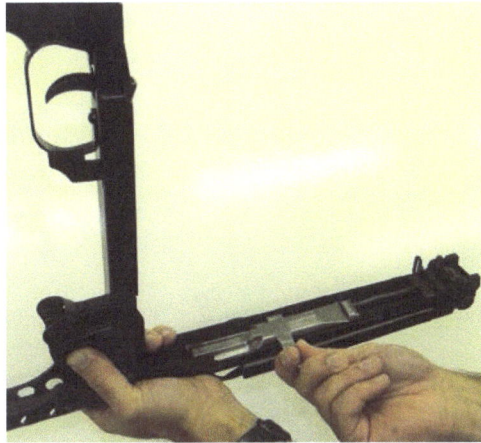

Figure 2-18

3. Once the bolt assembly is in the receiver channel, allow the spring to push the bolt forward while under your control; do not slam (Figure 2-18).

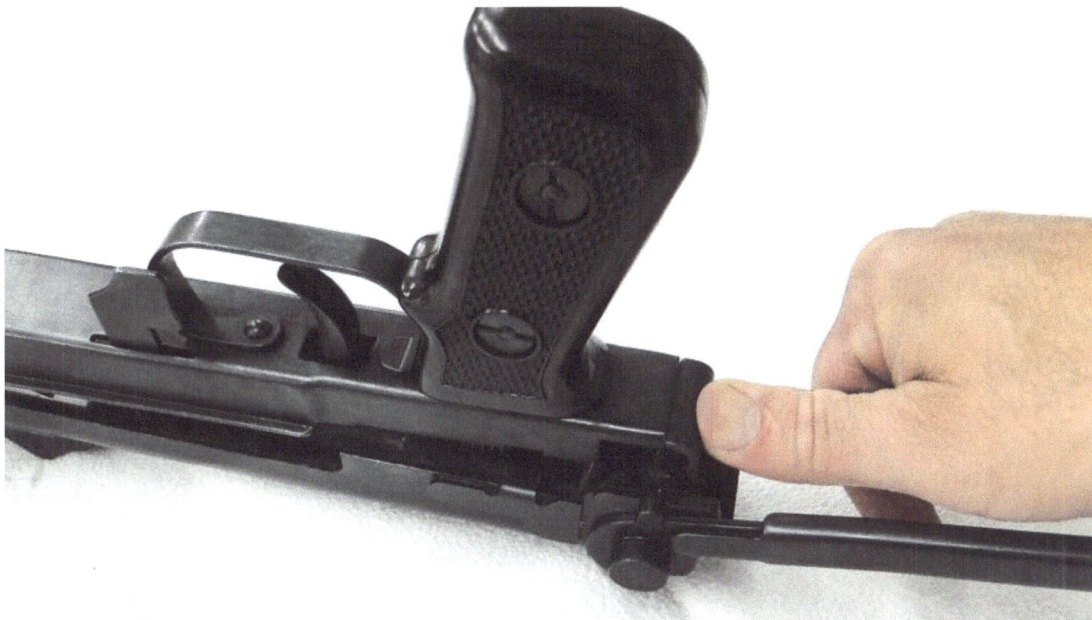

Figure 2-19

4. Rotate the lower receiver down to close the receiver until the receiver catch hood engages, pressing in the release to fully close (Figure 2-19).

Performing a Function Check on the PPS-43 SMG

NOTE- Ensure there is no magazine in the weapon; clear prior to performing a function check.

    A. Place the safety in the "FIRE" position.

    B. Pull the operating handle fully rearward and release it. Bolt should lock to the rear.

    C. Place the safety in the "SAFE" position.

    D. Press trigger. The bolt should not go forward.

    E. Push forward on the safety to place it on "FIRE".

    F. Press trigger and hold it to the rear. The bolt should go forward, and you can continue to cycle the action simulating full-automatic fire.

    G. Release the trigger, and the bolt should lock to the rear.

Section 3

Operation and Function

Loading the PPS-43 Stick Magazine

To load the column magazine

> 1. Grasp the magazine in the non-dominant hand with the mouth upward and the lug to the left, with several cartridges in the dominant hand.
>
> 2. Holding the next cartridge by the thumb and index finger of the dominant hand on the projectile and shoulder of the case, press down on the follower with the cartridge rim, and insert the cartridge under magazine lips with pressure of the thumb on the case shoulder.
>
> 3. Pick up the next cartridge in the same manner, and placing its rim on the cartridge just inserted into the magazine, insert this cartridge under the magazine lips.
>
> 4. Continue to load 35 cartridges into the magazine in the same manner.

Loading the Stick Magazine in a PPS-43 SMG

Figure 3-1

1. With the SMG pointed in a safe direction, bolt forward with the safety engaged, hold the pistol grip with the dominant hand and the stick magazine in the non-dominant hand (Figure 3-1).

Figure 3-2

2. Place the mouth of the magazine into the magazine well of the receiver so that the magazine slides into the receiver slot (Figure 3-2).

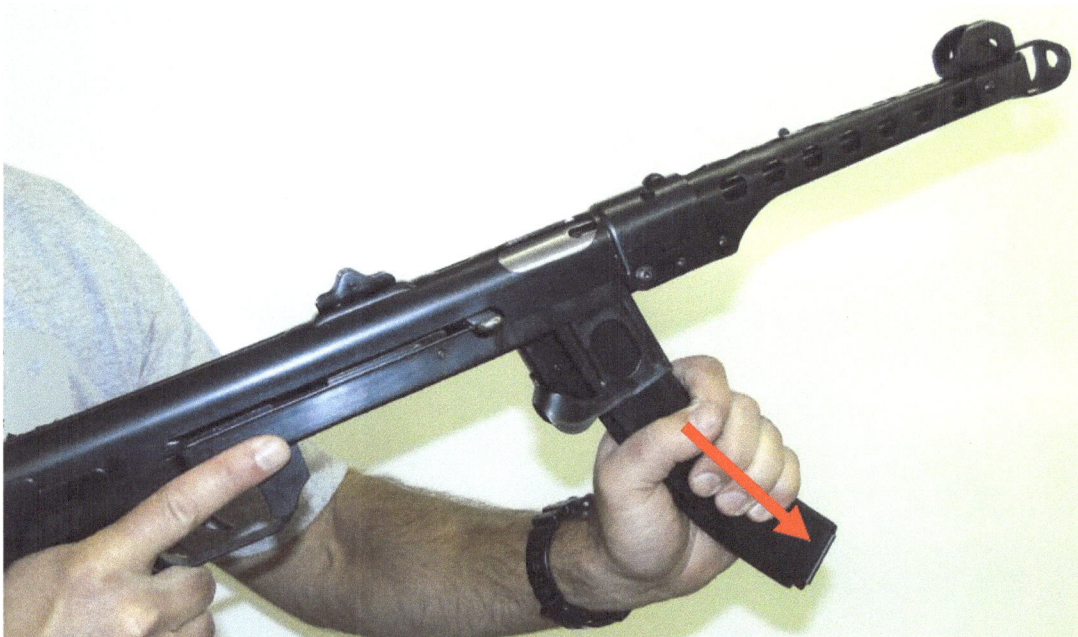

Figure 3-3

3. Ensure the magazine locks into the receiver by pulling it down; reinsert if the magazine is not locked into position (Figure 3-3).

Firing the PPS-43 SMG

Figure 3-4 RPG gunner with a PPS-43 in combat recently in the Ivory Coast

A. Orient downrange or towards the threat.

Figure 3-5a

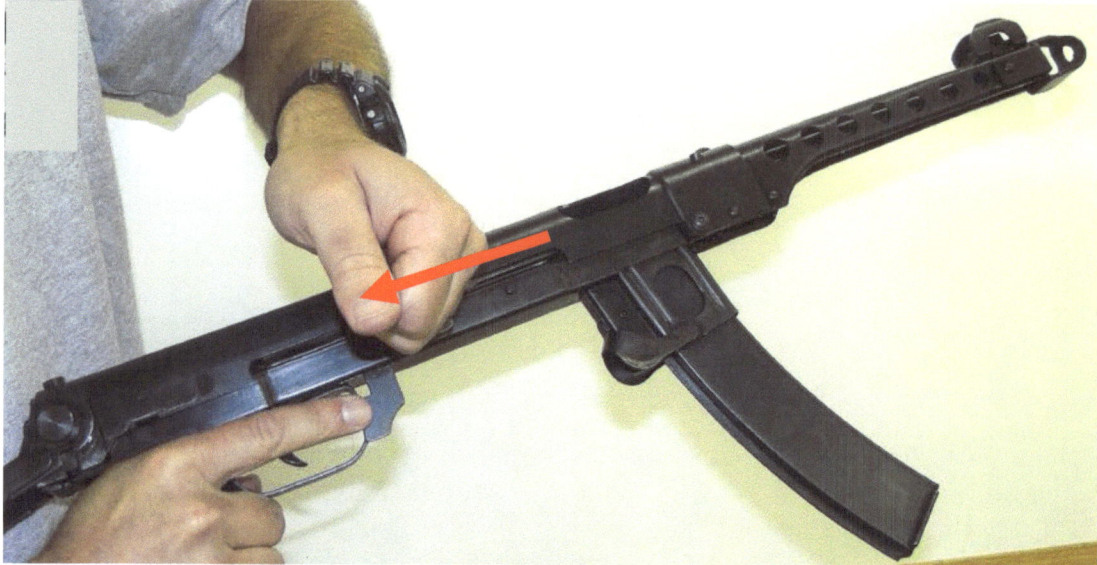

Figure 3-5b

B. If the bolt is forward and the safety engaged, you must press the safety forward to disengage (Figure 3-5a) and pull the bolt **fully** to the rear until it catches the sear (Figure 3-5b). Release the bolt and re-grip the weapon.

Figure 3-6

C. As you orient your sights onto the target, press the trigger straight back so as not to interrupt the sight picture (Figure 3-6). As the PPS-43 is an open-bolt weapon, you will notice the movement of the bolt forward once you press the trigger; take this movement into account to maintain your sight alignment and sight picture on the target.

D. For full-automatic bursts, press and hold the trigger to the rear for four- to six-round bursts and release to reacquire your sights on target. Continue to burst fire as the target requires.

Figure 3-7a Bolt to the rear   Figure 3-7b Bolt forward
PPS-43 SMG safety catch position SAFE

E. When you have completed firing the SMG, place the safety on "**SAFE**" position (Figures 3-7a and 3-7b).

F. You will notice upon firing your last cartridge that the bolt will not return to the rear and will remain forward. If you suspect it is due to a dud round, recharge the bolt to the rear and attempt to fire.

G. Once firing is completed, clear the weapon as previously detailed in Chapter 2.

Zeroing the PPS-43 SMG

Zero procedure: Attempt to do this on a known-distance range on a windless day from a solid bench rest.

Figure 3-8a 100 Meter sight setting   Figure 3-8b 200 Meter sight setting
Photos of the rear sight and protective sight wings

Figure 3-9a Top view   Figure 3-9b Side view
Photos of the front sight and protective sight hood

Sight adjustments are made to the front sight of the PPS-43 (Figures 3-9a and 3-9b).

The front sight consists of a rotating sight post. The front sight will allow you to adjust for elevation by rotating the front sight pin up or down. Note: If you wish to move your point of impact up, then you must rotate the sight down. If you wish your point of impact to go down, you must rotate the front-sight pin up. If you wish to change your windage, then you must drift the windage slide in the opposite direction desired. In general, any changes you make in your front sight must be made in the opposite direction.

Establish a Zero

- Distance to target should be 50 meters, and the sight should be set on "20" (for 200 meters).
- Target should be 12 inches/30 cm high by 8 inches/20 cm, roughly a piece of letter-sized paper on a target silhouette.
- From a bench or prone position with sandbags for support, carefully aim and fire four round bursts. Ensure proper sight alignment and sight picture and a straight back press of the trigger. If your shots are not striking the point-of-aim, then adjust your sights.
- To raise the next shot group, rotate the front-sight post in the down direction (clockwise).
- To lower the next shot group, rotate the front-sight post in the up direction (counter-clockwise).
- To move the next shot group left, drift the front sight to the right.
- To move the next shot group right, drift the front sight to the left.
- Continue to fire four-shot bursts and adjust the sights until you have at least a three out of four hits on the piece of paper.
- Once this step is done, the SMG is now combat-zeroed. Remember: All shots taken closer than 50 meters will be slightly high but not by more than 3" at extremely close ranges.
- Also remember the PPS-43 was designed to be a submachine gun, not a sniper rifle; group sizes will be looser than rifles.

Section 4

Performance Problems

Malfunction Procedures

Malfunctions are usually preventable through good practices, but they may still occur out of the blue from time to time. Of course, you hope it is on the practice range, but you should treat each one as if you are in a life-or-death situation. Practicing proper and effective corrective actions will allow you to be more confident in your weapon handling. In stressful situations, you can become much more stressed due to an unforeseen malfunction that is easy to correct. I have observed many shooters that perceive themselves to be experienced, but when they encounter a stovepipe, they nearly disassemble the weapon rather than sweep it out and continue.

Malfunction drills must fix the problem 100% of the time (excluding a weapon stoppage—broken weapon) the first time performed. You must look at the weapon and identify the problem (obviously the SMG is not functioning as you need, so you must transition to another weapon or rectify the situation). It is a non-functioning weapon at this point—fix it.

You should always practice taking a covered position to correct malfunctions with considerations on how you operate.

Malfunction	Probable Cause	Corrective Action
Cartridge stuck at chamber opening. Cartridge unfired. Bolt not fully forward. Cartridge not in chamber.	1. Magazine lips bent.	*Do not close bolt. Lock bolt back in rearward position. Remove magazine.*
	2. Recoil spring weak.	1. If unfired round was at an angle to the chamber opening, compare top round angle to that of top round in a good functioning magazine. Carefully bend the magazine feed lip(s) so both cartridge angles are identical. Reinsert and retry the previously non-functioning magazine.
	3. Magazine spring weakened.	2. If unfired round was in direct line with chamber and partially or fully chambered, then recoil spring is too weak. Replace spring.
	4. Drum spring tension needs adjustment.	
Round in chamber, unfired, light primer hit.	1. Weak recoil spring.	1. Replace recoil spring.
	2. Upper receiver bent or misaligned.	2. Have competent gunsmith bring upper receiver back to original position.
Spent shell casings not ejecting.	1. Worn or broken extractor.	1. Replace extractor.
	2. Cartridge support 'finger(s)' at bottom of bolt face broken.	2. Replace or re-weld bolt.
	3. Bent, worn or broken ejector.	3. Repair or replace ejector.
	4. Weak reloads.	4. If using reloads, make sure they are hot enough to eject shell at least 3 feet or 4 feet upward.
	5. Receiver bowed.	5."My gun was not ejecting spent cases all the time, and I found that the receiver was bowed from the chamber end of the barrel to the locking latch in the rear. The amount of bow was a little more than 1/8" and was letting the bolt ride too high in the receiver, missing the ejector on occasion. Made a jig in my shop to bring the receiver back to original shape and now the gun runs like a champ!"
Fires round(s) after trigger released.	1. Upper receiver raised slightly.	1. Only takes about 1/16" to 1/8" extra height between upper receiver and lower receiver for bolt to 'jump' over sear. Test by holding or taping down upper receiver and shooting weapon. If this cures the problem, then place spacer between upper receiver and receiver locking cover.
	2. Recoil spring not correct length or strength.	2. Replace recoil spring *(this cures a lot of functioning problems).*
	3. Worn trigger bar sear or cocking recess on bolt bottom.	3. Inspect trigger bar sear and bolt cocking recess for wear. Replace or repair as necessary.
	4. Broken or weak trigger bar spring.	4. Remove and disassemble trigger group. Inspect trigger bar spring. Replace spring if broken. Replacing with too strong a spring will cause bolt to stop while firing full auto.
Round in chamber, empty shell on top causing a jam.	This usually is caused by the extractor not holding the spent shell tightly enough when extracting.	Remove the leaf spring holding the extractor by pushing up on the extractor, which pushes up the spring and creates an opening. At the same time, place a small round object through the opening, thereby holding the spring slightly higher than the top of the extractor. Next, push the spring forward and out. The extractor can now be removed upward. Clean the extractor, and with a small pick, clean the grooves in which the extractor moves. Put back together and check the extractor tension by placing a fired shell in the bolt face and see if the extractor now holds the shell firmly.

Appendix A – Ammunition Specifics

7.62x25mm Tokarev

Figure A-1 Side-by-side comparison to other cartridges
From left: .45 ACP, 7.62x25mm Tokarev, 9 mm Luger, and 9x18mm Makarov

Figure A-2 7.62x25mm Tokarev rounds
Left: Standard FMJ. Right: Military armor-piercing round

Figure A-3 7.63x25mm Mauser round and 7.62x25mm Tokarev round

The **7.62x25 Tokarev** cartridge is a bottle-necked pistol cartridge widely used in former Soviet and Soviet satellite states. Actual caliber of the bullet is 7.85mm (.309 inches).

Design
The cartridge is basically a Soviet version of the 7.63mm Mauser. They are very similar; in fact, some weapons can use both cartridges interchangeably, though this is not recommended. 7.62 Tokarev is usually much more powerful than its Mauser counterpart and can damage any firearms chambered for 7.63mm Mauser. The Czech version of this cartridge has a 25% higher pressure loading, meaning that it produces significantly more velocity and energy than other common loads and may present a danger to the user when fired from weapons not specifically designed to use it.

The Soviets produced a wide array of loadings for this cartridge for use in submachine guns. These include armor-piercing, tracer, and incendiary rounds. This cartridge has excellent penetration and can defeat lighter ballistic vests (class I and II). Although most firearms chambered in this caliber were declared obsolete and removed from military inventories, some Russian police and Special Forces units still use it for its superior penetration, rather than the more popular 9mm Makarov ammunition in current use.

Some firearms that use this round are pistols Tokarev TT-33 and Vz 52 and submachine guns PPD-40, PPSh-41, PPS-43, and K-50 m.

Reloaders have been known to custom load 7.62x25mm with .30 caliber sabot rounds with .22 caliber 55 grain (3.6 g) bullets. Muzzle velocities in excess of 2200 ft/s (670 m/s) have been obtained with this method. These speeds are seldom obtained with a handgun; usually, the longer barrel of a rifle is required.

Synonyms
- 7.62mm Type P
- 7.62mm Tokarev
- 7.62x25mm Tokarev
- 7.62x25mm TT
- .30 Tokarev

7.62mm cartridges, type 1930, with a regular bullets
- 7.63mm, Mauser, made in a cartridge factory in the city of Podolsk at the end of the 1920s. The prototype of the cartridge, type 1930.
- 7.62mm, type 1930, lead core and bimetallic-jacketed bullet. Cartridge case - brass.
- 7.62mm, type 1930, lead core and steel-jacketed bullet. Cartridge case - brass. WWII production.
- 7.62mm, type 1930, lead core and steel-jacketed bullet. Cartridge case - steel. WWII production.

- 7.62mm, type 1930, lead core and bimetallic-jacketed bullet. Cartridge case - bimetallic. WWII production.
- 7.62mm, type 1930, with lead core and steel-jacketed bullet. Cartridge case-steel, brass.
- 7.62mm, type 1930, with lead core and bimetallic jacketed bullet. Cartridge case - bimetallic. Production in the 1950s.

7.62mm cartridges, type 1930, with special bullets
- 7.62mm, type 1930 with armor-piercing + incendiary by bullet P-41. Cartridge case - brass.
- 7.62mm, type 1930 with a tracer bullet. Cartridge case - brass. Production period of WWII.
- 7.62mm, type 1930 with a tracer bullet. Cartridge case - brass. Production end of the '40s.
- 7.62mm, type 1930 with a tracer bullet. The case - bimetallic. Produced up to the 50s.

Auxiliary cartridges
- 7.62mm, type 1930. Dummy cartridge. Made up to the end of the 1940s.
- 7.62mm, type 1930. Cartridge case - brass. Dummy cartridge. Production in the '50s.
- 7.62mm, type 1930. Cartridge case - bimetallic. Dummy cartridge. Production in the '50s.
- 7.62mm, type 1930. Technological.
- 7.62mm, type 1930. Cartridge case - brass. Blank cartridge.
- 7.62mm, type 1930. Cartridge case - bimetallic. Blank cartridge.

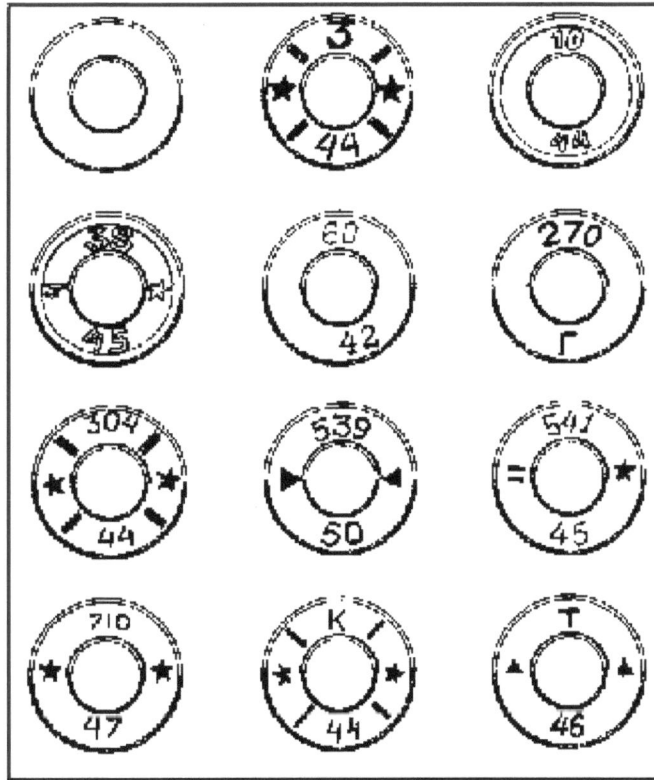

Figure A-4 Factory head stamps

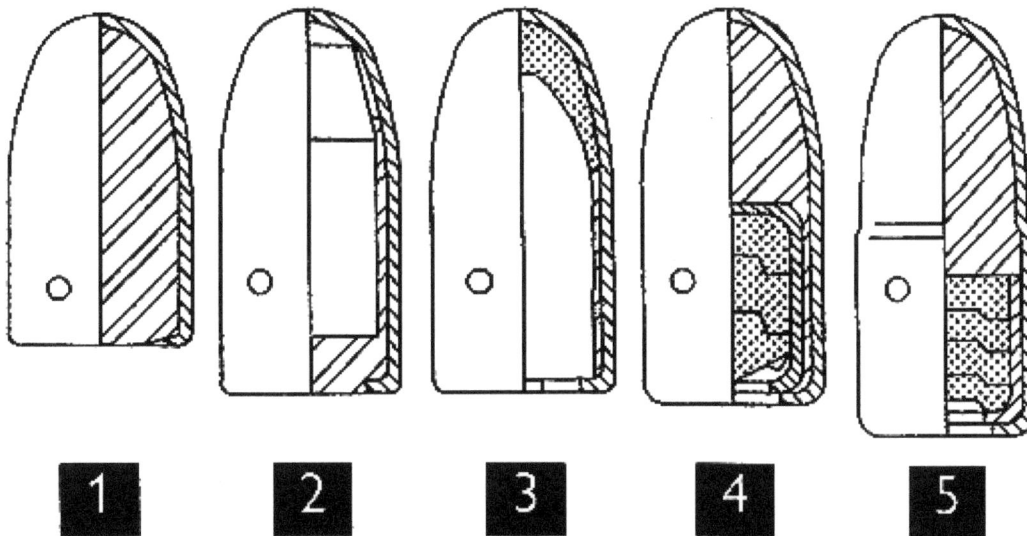

Figure A-5 Sectional view of bullets

1. Regular bullet with the lead core "P"
2. Regular bullet with the steel core "Pst"
3. Armor-piercing + incendiary bullet "P-41"
4. Tracer bullet "PT" (production in the 1940s)
5. Tracer bullet "PT" (production in the 1950s)

At the end of the 1920s, there was a need by the Red Army for a new type of pistol. The alternative between pistols and revolvers was already settled in favor of the pistol. Together with weapon types of diverse design (starting from original models of the designers Korovin, Prilutsky, Tokarev and foreign pistols Mauser, Walther and Steyr) domestic versions of ammunition were tested. The cartridge plant in city Podolsk, at this time, made a small amount of cartridges for the pistols Browning, Mauser, Steyr, and some other models. After testing for a standard round, the Mauser cartridge, caliber 7.63mm, was selected for use in a new pistol. Most likely, the purchase had important value for the weapons of the NKVD (People's Commissariat of Internal Affairs), who had plenty of 7.63mm Mauser pistols. For standardization with the existing ammunition caliber, the cartridge was changed to 7.62mm, though the tolerances of the cartridge case and bullet practically had not changed. As for the first cartridges being a copy of the 7.63mm Mauser cartridge, the new 7.62mm ammunition received a bullet of greater diameter than the cartridge of the Nagant revolver, and more ductility of the case, thus permitting the increase of the force of ejection with automatic weapons. The bullet exterior - increase of radius/ogive had also changed, making its nose cone longer, as contrasted to the prototype. With these changes, this ammo was adopted by the Red Army under the title - "7.62mm, cartridge for pistols, type 1930."

The difficulties which arose with the development of the pistol "TT" were mirrored in the quantity of ammunition issued for it. Prior to the beginning of the Great Patriotic War, the production of cartridges for TT was limited to a rather small amount. On the cartridge cases made in this period, head stamps are absent. The cartridges were produced only with a regular lead core bullet. The bullet jacket was usually steel, with a tombac plating (an alloy of copper and zinc). A powder charge weight was selected using a calculation for obtaining, at 10 meters, a muzzle velocity of 420-450 mps. It gave a bullet energy of 2070 kg, at the same distance, equal to 60 kg/m, at a mean maximum pressure, which was not superior. The mean charge weight of P-45/1 smokeless powder (porous), depending on a consignment, lag within the limits of 0.48 - 0.52 grams. This was applied to equipment and the "VP" powder (Viscose, for Pistols), whose weight oscillated from 0.48 up to 0.6 grams. The grain of the powder P-45/1, was a dark-green color in the form of a short, rather thick cylinder, whereas the grain "VP" represents a thin, long cylinder of greenish color. This powder was used in cartridges made until 1946. The production of this ammunition was sharply increased in the '40s with the beginning of the mass issuing of SMGs.

In 1941, for the SMG, the cartridge with the "P-41" bullet was introduced into the inventory. The cartridge came with an armor-piercing + incendiary bullet and well-tried steel core -- for defeating enemy personnel, for firing at petrol tanks, motorcycles, automobiles, and airplanes.

The "P-41" bullet, with a weight of 4.3 – 5.1 grams, had a black tip with a red band.

In 1943, a cartridge with tracer bullet "PT," with a weight of 5.2 - 5.5 grams, was also produced. It gave a bright red line at distances up to 400 meters and was used for indicating targets in combat. The cupola of a bullet was green in color. The new plants, in addition, were attracted to production of cartridges with a regular bullet, and since 1942, placed a head stamp of the manufacturer and year of issue on the cartridge case. And, since 1944, when the productivity of the plants reached a maximum, large plants, in addition to using steel, put the month of manufacturing on the cartridge. Smaller plants put the quarter date of manufacture on the cartridge case. The increase in the issue of ammunition demanded plenty of scarce materials: brass for cartridge cases and bimetal for manufacturing shell cases. On the other hand, observance of specifications was not required for rigid long-term ammunition storage - they immediately went to the regular army. Such a situation allowed materials to be partially substituted. Four plants out of eight releasing this category of ammunition had run in production cartridges with cheaper bimetallic cartridge cases, and occasionally also steel cartridge cases without a coating. There were bullets with a steel jacket without a coating or plated by brass instead of tombac. Engaging new plants in the manufacturing of cartridges, prior to releasing ammunition and usage of simplified military technologies, lowered the quality of production. Later, once after the end of the WWII, the remaining ammunition issued up to 1946 was practically completely given away to troops for practice firing or was destroyed. In the post-war time, the production quotas of ammunition were sharply reduced, many plants starting peace production. Because of reduction of deliveries of a bimetal until 1949, the cartridge was produced only with a brass cartridge case. As of 1949, there was a steel brass cartridge case, the production of which was finished by 1952 with restoration of the issue of bimetallic cartridge cases, soon completely superseding brass. At the same time, modifications were made in the design of a tracer bullet.

The last modernization of the cartridge was in 1955, when instead of the old lead-core bullet, a new one was adopted with the cheaper and solid steel core. For preservation of the former weight, the length of a bullet was increased up to 16.5 mm. Since 1951, the new bullet, step-by-step, replaced, at miscellaneous plants, production of the old bullet. Except for battle cartridges, cartridges of a secondary role were also produced. During the post-war years, blank cartridges appeared. Instead of a bullet, it had an elongated cartridge case pressed into a "star." Dummy cartridges made prior to the beginning of the '50s differed from battle ammo by two or three cross-sectional flutes on the cartridge case. Later, cross-sectional flutes were changed to four longitudinal flutes. The corporations - developers of rifle weapons for the needs -- produced mock-up cartridges from battle cartridges, minus the powder, left with the subsequent coating of the cartridge with nickel or cadmium.

A cartridge case with a charge and paper wad instead of a bullet was applied as a burster charge to the flame-thrower ROKS-2. (The wad and bottom of the case were covered with red lacquer for differentiation.)

The gradual replacement at the end of the 1950s of the TT pistols with the PM and APS pistols, and also SMGs by AK-47s, at first decreased, and then, in general, eliminated the necessity for production of the 7.62x25mm cartridge. However, equipment for production was saved at plant 38 until 1989. In the 1970s and in the beginning of the 1980s, special lots of cartridges were produced, on orders of the Army, for export and for certain organizations.

For difference, the cupola of a bullet of such a cartridge was colored white. In 1985, the last consignment of tracer cartridges, were probably exported. From 1965 till 1973 and from 1982-1986, by the order of film studios, plant #38 made a significant amount of blank cartridges of miscellaneous designs except for the standard version, with a brass case length of 34 mm, and the so-called "universal" cartridge, with a bimetallic case length of 29 mm. This blank cartridge was used to fire from weapons using the 7.62 TT cartridge and 9mm "Parabellum" and 9mm "Makarov."

The history of this cartridge is far from completion. Probably, it will become the basis for creation of modern types of rifles. Confirmation to that is the mention of the 7.62x25mm cartridge in the program for creation of a prospective pistol for the Russian Army. The interest in the 7.62x25mm cartridge is exhibited by the Ministry of Internal Affairs. Reasons to this are twofold. On the one hand, the widespread occurrence of a means of individual protection has considerably lowered the efficiency 9mm of the cartridge Makarov. On the other hand, in military warehouses, there are huge reserves of 7.62mm cartridges. This fact is especially significant for modern economic considerations.

(From the Russian magazine **MasterGun** *[МАСТЕР-РУЖЬЕ] #7/8, 1996)*

Appendix B - Ammunition Comparison

9x18mm
Makarov

9x19mm
Luger

7.62x25mm
Tokarev

.45 ACP

PISTOLS AND SUBMACHINE GUNS

Size Comparison of NATO vs. Non-Standard Ammunition

5.56x
45mm

5.45x
39mm

5.56x
45mm

7.62x
39mm

7.62x
51mm

7.62x
54R mm

12.7x
99mm

12.7x
108mm

ASSAULT RIFLES

SNIPER RIFLES & MACHINE GUNS

Appendix C - Non-Standard Ammunition Packaging & Markings

Packaging

Russian small arms cartridges are packed in sealed sheet-metal containers, with two containers per wooden crate. Older Russian production used rectangular containers of heavy gauge galvanized iron with soldered seams. Around 1959, the introduction of painted, rolled edge, rounded corner, tin plate 'sardine can' containers became the standard.

Metal and wooden crates have standardized markings that identify the contents as to caliber, functional type, cartridge case material, quantity and cartridge/powder lot data. Specialized cartridges are further identified by a color code consisting of one or two color stripes which correspond to bullet tip color. AP cartridges with tungsten carbide cores are identified by two concentric circles instead of color stripes. Russian cartridge designation, packaging and marking practices are generally followed by former Soviet-Bloc countries; each, however, has introduced some modifications in designation and marking. Russian ammunition packaging can be distinguished from Bulgarian packaging, which also carries Cyrillic markings, primarily by the different factory codes. The factory code on the container also appears in the headstamp of the cartridges in the container.

Steel Ammo Tins
(Sardine Cans)

Wood Ammo Crate (Case)
(Contains 2 Tins + Opener)

Cartridge quantities and weights of wooden crates

Country	Manufacturer	Caliber	Rounds /Crate	Crate Weight
Czech Rep.	Sellier and Bellot	14.5 x 114	210	53 kg.
India	OFB	14.5 x 114	60	15.5 kg.
Russia	Unknown	14.5 x 114	80	23 kg.
Bulgaria	Arsenal	12.7 x 108	200	29 kg.
Bulgaria	Arsenal	12.7 x 108	200	32 kg.
Pakistan	POF	12.7 x 108	280	42 kg.
Russia	Unknown	12.7 x 108	190	29 kg.
Russia	Novosibirsk	12.7 x 108	160	25 kg.
Bulgaria	Arsenal	7.62 x 54(R)	880	25 kg.
Czech Rep.	Sellier and Bellot	7.62 x 54(R)	800	24 kg.
Russia	Novosibirsk	7.62 x 54(R)	880	26 kg.
Russia	Novosibirsk	7.62 x 54(R)	600	21 kg.
Russia	Unknown	7.62 x 54(R)	880	26 kg.
Serbia	Prvi Partizan	7.62 x 54(R)	1,200	39 kg.
Czech Rep.	Sellier and Bellot	7.62 x 39	1,200	28 kg.
Pakistan	POF	7.62 x 39	1,750	39 kg.
Russia	Barnaul	7.62 x 39	1,320	30 kg.
Serbia	Prvi Partizan	7.62 x 39	1,260	29 kg.
Sudan	STC	7.62 x 39	1,500	28.1 kg.
Ukraine	Lugansk	7.62 x 39	1,320	30 kg.
Yugoslavia	Igman Zavod	7.62 x 39	1,260	28 kg.
Yugoslavia	Igman Zavod	7.62 x 39	1,120	27.5 kg.
Russia	Unknown	5.45 x 39	2,160	29 kg.
Ukraine	Lugansk	5.45 x 39	2,160	29 kg.

Non-Standard Ammunition tin and crate marking - diagrams

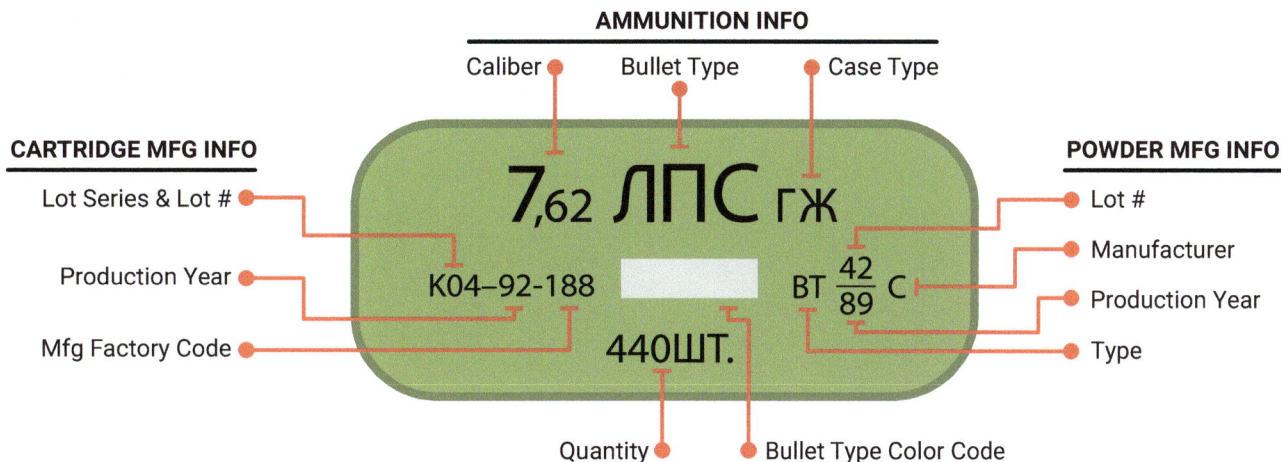

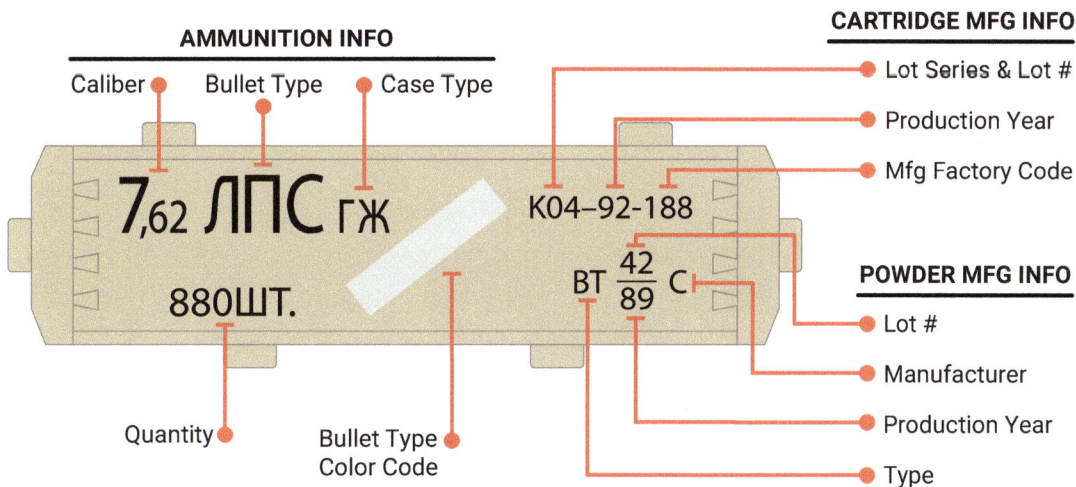

AMMUNITION INFO

Caliber — Bullet Type — Case Type

CARTRIDGE MFG INFO
- Lot Series & Lot #
- Production Year
- Mfg Factory Code

POWDER MFG INFO
- Lot #
- Manufacturer
- Production Year
- Type

$$7{,}62 \; \text{ЛПС} \; \text{ГЖ}$$

K04–92–188

BT $\frac{42}{89}$ C

440ШТ.

Quantity — Bullet Type Color Code

AMMUNITION INFO

Caliber — Bullet Type — Case Type

CARTRIDGE MFG INFO
- Lot Series & Lot #
- Production Year
- Mfg Factory Code

POWDER MFG INFO
- Lot #
- Manufacturer
- Production Year
- Type

$$7{,}62 \; \text{ЛПС} \; \text{ГЖ}$$

880ШТ.

K04–92–188

BT $\frac{42}{89}$ C

Quantity — Bullet Type Color Code

Non-Standard Ammunition tin and crate marking - Russian ammunition data

CASE TYPE MARKINGS

Mark	Meaning
ГЖ	Bimetallic case (gilding metal clad steel)
ГЛ	Brass case
ГС	Steel case

CARTRIDGE MFG FACTORY CODES

Code	Location
3	Ulyanovsk
17	Barnaul
38	Yuryuzan
60	Frunze (now Bishkek)
188	Novosibirsk
270	Voroshilovgrad (now Luhansk)
304	Lugansk
539	Tula
711	Klimovsk
T	Tula

Non-Standard Ammunition tin and crate marking - Russian ammunition data

BULLET TYPE MARKINGS

Mark	Meaning
Б Б-30 Б-32 БП	Armor-piercing
Б3	Armor-piercing incendiary
Б3Т Б3Т-44	Armor-piercing incendiary tracer
БС БС-40 БС-41	Armor-piercing with special core of tungsten carbide instead of carbon steel
БСТ	Armor-piercing with tungsten carbide core with added tracer
БТ	Armor-piercing tracer
Д	Heavy (long-range) with lead core instead of carbon steel
З ЗП	Incendiary
Л	Lightweight bullet
ЛПС	Light ball bullet with mild steel core
МДЗ	High explosive incendiary
П П-41	Spotting / ranging
П3	Incendiary spotting / ranging
ПП	Enhanced penetration
ПС	Spotting / ranging with mild steel core
ПТ	Spotting / ranging tracer
СНБ	Armor-piercing sniper
Т Т-30 Т-45 Т-46	Tracer
57-У-322 57-У-323	Cartridge with higher powder charge
57-У-423	High-pressure cartridge
57-Х-322 57-Х-323 57-Х-340	Blank cartridge
57-НЕ-УЧ	Training cartridge
7Н1	Sniper bullet

BULLET TYPE COLOR CODES (Ammunition up to 14.5mm)

Color	Meaning
No color	Ball
White tip	Reference Ball
Silver tip	Light ball with steel core
Yellow tip	Heavy ball, or ball with torpedo base (on 7.62x54R)
Blue tip + white band	Short range ball 14.5x114 (only Hungarian and Czech)
Green tip + white band	Short range, tracer, (only Czech designation, only found on 7.62x39 with round nose)
Green tip	Tracer
Green tip & headstamp or entire cartridge green	Subsonic ammunition for silencer-weapons
Red tip	Spotting charge, incendiary
Red tip + white band	Short range tracer ball 14.5x114 (only Hungarian designation)
Entire bullet red	High explosive bullet (7.62x54R after 1945)
Entire bullet red	High explosive bullet (on 12.7 and 14.5mm)
Magenta tip + red band	Armor piercing incendiary tracer
Black tip + red band	Armor piercing incendiary
Black tip + red shell	Armor piercing incendiary with tungsten carbide core
Black tip + yellow band	Armor piercing incendiary Phosphorus 12.7
Black tip	Armor piercing

** The bullet tip color codes in the table above will be the same color codes on the tins or crates, but they will be color stripes on the packaging.

Example:

CARTRIDGE
Black Tip + Red Band

TIN or CRATE
Black Stripe + Red Stripe

Appendix D - Non-Standard Weapon Identification Markings

General Identification Markings

There are various identification markings found on non-standard weapons. Typically the markings will provide some or all of the following information:
- factory name or stamp (proof mark)
- caliber & serial number
- selector lever markings/symbols
- rear sight mark/symbol

Selector Lever Markings on Kalashnikov Rifles

Upper/ Safe Symbol	Mid/ Full-Auto Symbol	Lower/ Semi-Auto Symbol	Country
	Д	1	Albania
	L	D	Albania
	AB	ЕД	Bulgaria
	L	D	China
	进	单	China
	30	1	Czechoslovakia
	آلـ	فردى	Egypt
	D	E	Egypt
	D	E	East Germany
	∞	1	Hungary
آ	ص	م	Iraq
	련	단	North Korea
	C	P	Poland
	Z	O	Poland
S	A	R	Romania
S	FA	FF	Romania
	1	3	Romania
	ЛР	ОГОНЬ	Russia
	АВ	ОД	Russia
U	R	Ј	Yugo/Serbia

Rear Sight Marks on Kalashnikov Rifles

Symbol	Country
D	Albania
П	Bulgaria
D	China
N	East Germany
A	Hungary
订	North Korea
S	Poland
P	Romania
П	Russia
O	Yugo/Serbia

NOTE: Data tables are not all inclusive, but they cover the more common weapon manufacturers.

Non-Standard Weapon Identification Markings

Factory Stamps and Countries of Manufacture

The table of symbols below are factory stamps (proof marks) for non-standard weapons. The symbols will identify the country of manufacture of the weapon. *NOTE: This is not an all inclusive list, but it covers the more common weapon manufacturers.*

(10) Bulgaria	(21) Bulgaria	(25) Bulgaria	China
(386) China	36 China	66 China	China
Egypt	East Germany	(3) East Germany	(K3) East Germany
East Germany	(06) East Germany	Iraq	Iraq
North Korea	North Korea	(11) Poland	Romania
Russia	Russia	Russia	Russia
Russia	Russia	Russia	Russia
Yugoslavia/Serbia	M.70.AB2 Yugoslavia/Serbia	ZASTAVA-KRAGUJEVAC Yugoslavia/Serbia	

Appendix E - Non-standard weapons theory overview

There are three key concepts to understand when manipulating non-standard weapons. These simple and logical concepts are:

1. CYCLE OF OPERATIONS
2. OPERATING SYSTEMS
3. LOCKING SYSTEMS

> Firearm design trends are shared across region, manufacturer and class of weapon and are relatively obvious to recognize.
>
> Keep in mind that firearms are essentially simple machines that harness the energy created by the fired cartridge to operate the system.

CYCLE OF OPERATIONS (COO)

The cycle of operations is a crucial basis for understanding how the weapon operates and for function/malfunction diagnosis. Each specific malfunction will correspond to a specific step or sometimes two in the COO. A failure in the system at a certain point, will by default, cause a failure of omission of all subsequent steps. (example – a failure to properly extract will manifest as a failure to eject.)

The COO will vary based on the type of operating and locking systems. Once the operating and locking systems of the weapon are known, the COO is logical.

The examples below all start from a standard reference point: the weapon is loaded, charged, placed on fire and the trigger is pulled.

'Cycle of Operations' Examples:

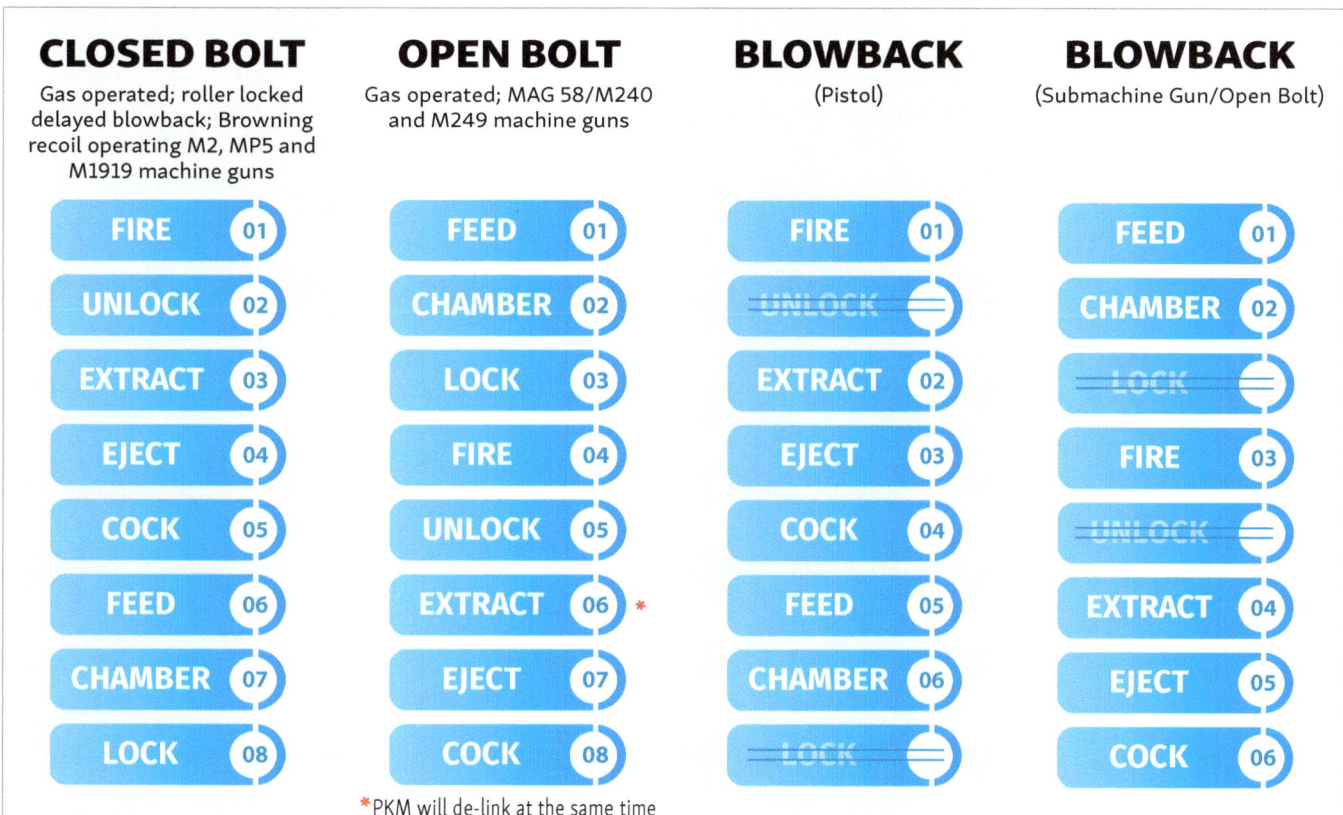

CLOSED BOLT	OPEN BOLT	BLOWBACK	BLOWBACK
Gas operated; roller locked delayed blowback; Browning recoil operating M2, MP5 and M1919 machine guns	Gas operated; MAG 58/M240 and M249 machine guns	(Pistol)	(Submachine Gun/Open Bolt)
FIRE 01	FEED 01	FIRE 01	FEED 01
UNLOCK 02	CHAMBER 02	~~UNLOCK~~	CHAMBER 02
EXTRACT 03	LOCK 03	EXTRACT 02	~~LOCK~~
EJECT 04	FIRE 04	EJECT 03	FIRE 03
COCK 05	UNLOCK 05	COCK 04	~~UNLOCK~~
FEED 06	EXTRACT 06 *	FEED 05	EXTRACT 04
CHAMBER 07	EJECT 07	CHAMBER 06	EJECT 05
LOCK 08	COCK 08	~~LOCK~~	COCK 06

*PKM will de-link at the same time

Non-standard weapons theory overview *(continued ...)*

⚙ OPERATING SYSTEMS

1. **Direct Impingement**- a type of gas operation that directs gas from a fired cartridge directly to the bolt carrier or slide assembly to cycle the action. (AR-15/M4 variants)

2. **Long-stroke piston system**- the piston is mechanically fixed to the bolt group and moves through the entire operating cycle. (AK variants)

3. **Short-stroke piston system (tappet system)**- the piston moves separately from the bolt group. It may directly push the bolt group parts as n the M1 carbine or operate through a connecting rod. (HK 416, AR180, POF, LWRC, FN FAL)

4. **Blowback**- the system of operation for self-loading firearms that obtains energy from the motion of the cartridge case as it is pushed to the rear by expanding gases created by the ignition of the propellant charge. (STEN, Makarov, M3 Grease Gun)

5. **Short recoil action**- the barrel and slide recoil only a short distance before they unlock and separate. The barrel stops quickly, and the slide continues rearward compressing the recoil spring and performing extraction, ejection and finally feeding a fresh round from the magazine in the counter recoil phase. During the last portion of its forward travel, the slide locks into the barrel and pushes the barrel back into battery. *(This is found in most handguns chambered for 9x19mm Parabellum or greater caliber. Smaller calibers, 9x18mm Makarov and below, generally use the blowback method of operation due to lower chamber pressure and associated simplicity of design.)

6. **Roller-locked, delayed-blowback**- when the bolt is closed, the rollers carried in the bolt are wedged into the receiver recesses. On firing, the rollers must be forced out of the recesses at great mechanical disadvantage, delaying the opening of the bolt, even with full power 7.62mm NATO (.308 Winchester) rifle cartridges used in the G3/HK 91 (G3, HK 91, HK 93, HK 53, MP5 variants)

7. **Inertia operated systems**- the bolt body is separated from the locked bolt body to remain stationary while the recoiling gun and locked bolt head moves rearward. This movement compresses the spring between the bolt head and bolt body, storing the energy required to cycle the action. Benelli shotguns.

Non-standard weapons theory overview *(continued ...)*

🔒 LOCKING SYSTEMS

1. **None** - all blowback pistols and some submachine guns – (STEN, UZI, M3 Grease Gun, Makarov, and CZ 82)

2. **Roller** - (HK variants, MG3, MG34, MG 42 and CZ 52)

3. **Rotating bolt** - (AK, Stoner, M60, and M249)

4. **Tilting bolt** - (SKS, FN FAL and MAG 58/M240)

5. **Tilting barrel** - (Tokarev TT33, Sig variants, M1911 variants and Glock variants)

6. **Rotating barrel** - (MAB P15, Colt All American 2000, and Beretta 8000)

7. **Locking flaps** - (RPD, DP/DPM and DShK)

8. **Falling locking block** - (P38, M9, and VZ58)

Function check
Checking the mechanical function of a weapon by replicating, without ammunition, the firing modes from the lowest rate of fire (SAFE if applicable) to the highest in a progressive sequence (not by selector location). The parts checked are the safety/safeties, sear and disconnector.

M4A1
1. Ensure the rifle is clear
2. Charge and place the weapon on SAFE
3. Attempt to fire (weapons should not FIRE, safety is functioning)
4. Place the weapon on SEMI, pull the trigger and hold it to the rear (hammer should fall, trigger/sear functioning)
5. Maintain the trigger to the rear and cycle the bolt
6. Release the trigger and listen for a metallic click (disconnector functioning)
7. Pull the trigger again and the hammer should fall
8. Charge the weapon and place on AUTO
9. Pull the trigger and hold it to the rear then cycle the bolt more than once
10. Release the trigger and pull it again, nothing should happen (auto sear is functioning)
11. Charge the weapon then pull the trigger again and the hammer should fall
12. Function check complete

Significant visual indicators
- Any checked, knurled or serrated surface
- Any movable lever or switch
- Pins with gripping surfaces
- Index marks (two lines that need to be aligned to disassembled (CZ 75)
- Recoil spring with ends of different diameters

www.ingramcontent.com/pod-product-compliance
Lightning Source LLC
Chambersburg PA
CBHW061057090426

42742CB00002B/72